I0815979

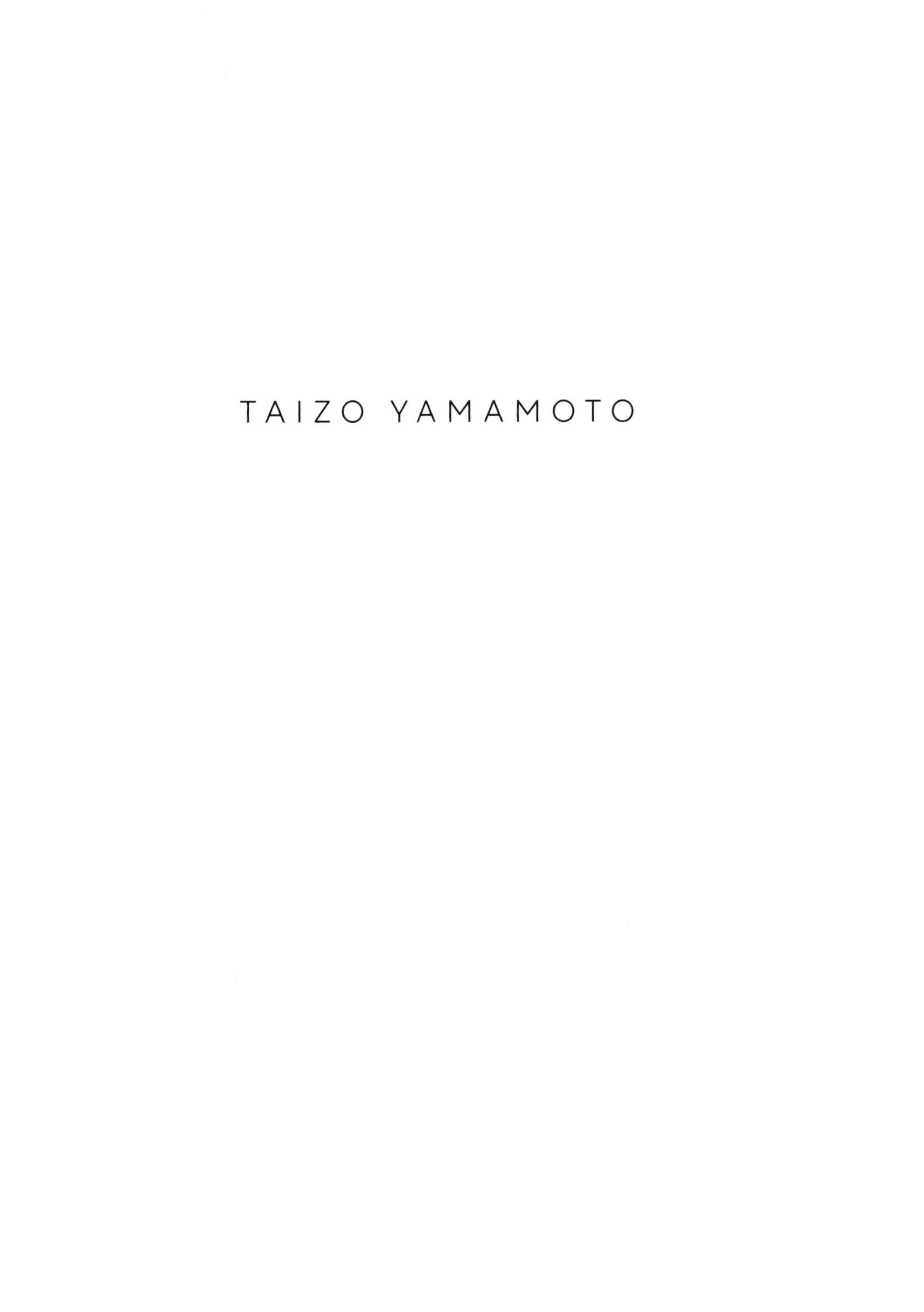

TAIZO YAMAMOTO

TAIZO YAMAMOTO

# CARTS
# HEDGES
# LIONS

Figure.1
*Vancouver / Toronto / Berkeley*

# CONTENTS

# PREFACE

**THIS COLLECTION OF DRAWINGS** records seemingly mundane and often overlooked subjects within Vancouver's city fabric. As a series, each group of drawings suggests recurring typologies and forms a kind of field guide through which to view the city. Context is removed from the drawings to emphasize the subject and to allow for easy comparison between occurrences, while the specificity of each subject refocuses attention to its singular moment. Each series considers different expressions related to ideas of home within Vancouver's changing and increasingly unaffordable landscape.

The drawings are made from photographs that capture the subjects in a split second. A meticulous accumulation of marks then remakes the image. The painstaking drawing process re-evaluates the instantaneous capture of the image and the incidental nature of the subject.

**SHOPPING CARTS** (2005-2008) documents sculptures of endless variation born from immediacy and necessity. Some carts are piled high with articles of weather protection, trade, and personal use, while others are almost empty. The carts are perpetual works-in-progress that offer momentary glimpses into the lives of their owners.

**HEDGES** (2008-2009) illustrates fences and hedges on Vancouver's arterial streets that shield homes from traffic and noise: nature enlisted as protection. These homes and hedges are slowly disappearing as single-family lots are assembled for construction of townhouses and apartments. The hedges display different attitudes toward growth, with some trees left to grow naturally and some pruned in more or less successful attempts at control.

**LION GATES** (2023-2024) records aspirational adornments to modest houses—gestures that connect notions of home across cultural boundaries. Pairs of cast-concrete sculptural lions stand in contrast to thin, decorative metal gates and utilitarian brick posts. These combinations of prefabricated elements become specific and personal expressions of each home, invoking the belief that each home needs a bit of protection and luck.

MANTIQUE

# SHOPPING CARTS

2005–2008

SHOPPING CART #4

Graphite on Bristol paper | 133 × 127 mm

SHOPPING CART #2

Graphite on Bristol paper | 165 × 152 mm

SHOPPING CART #7

Graphite on Bristol paper | 171 × 165 mm

MANTIQUE

SHOPPING CART #3

Graphite on Bristol paper | 140 × 127 mm

SHOPPING CART #11

Graphite on Bristol paper | 191 × 184 mm

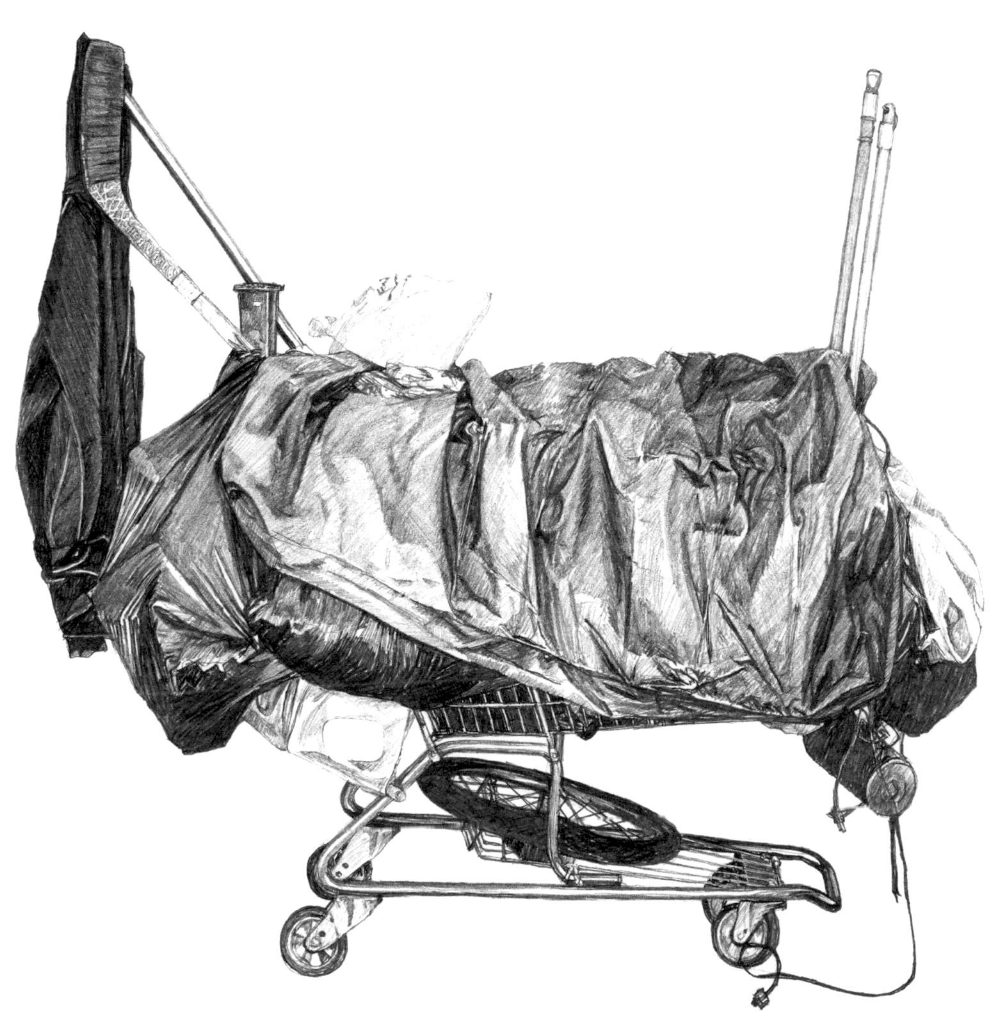

SHOPPING CART #8

Graphite on Bristol paper | 165 × 197 mm

SHOPPING CART #1

Graphite and pencil crayon on Bristol paper | 146 × 140 mm

SHOPPING CART #6

Graphite on Bristol paper | 171 × 152 mm

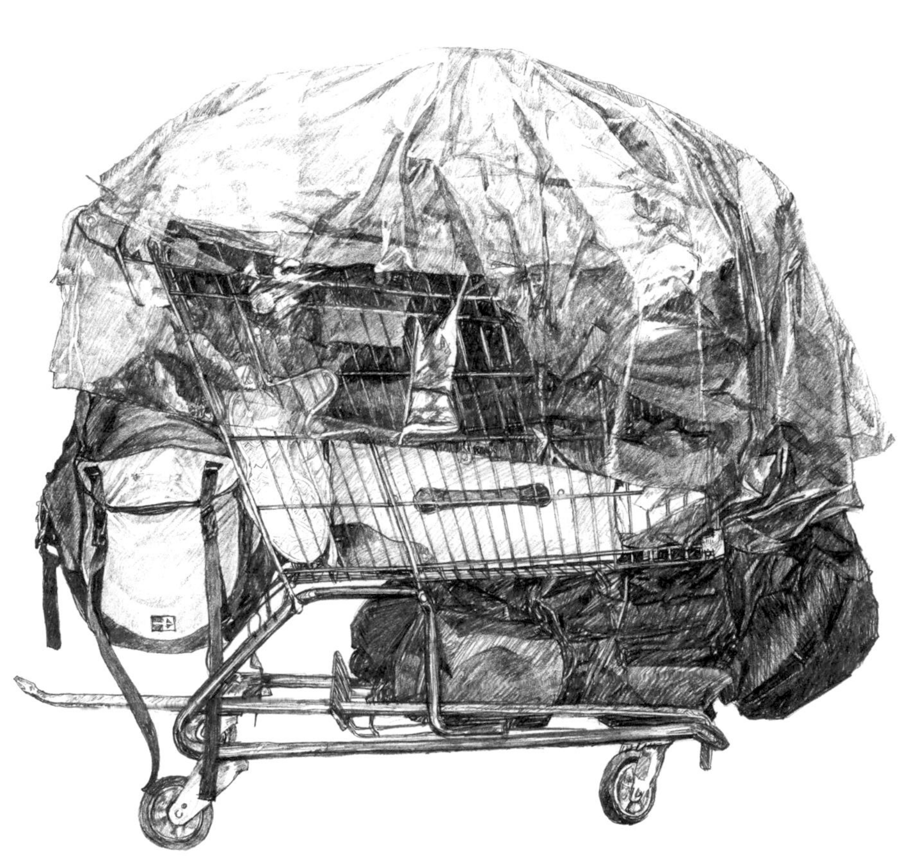

SHOPPING CART #10

Graphite on Bristol paper | 140 × 178 mm

SHOPPING CART #5

Graphite on Bristol paper | 171 × 152 mm

SHOPPING CART #16

Graphite on Bristol paper | 178 × 133 mm

**SHOPPING CART #20**

Graphite on Bristol paper | 178 × 127 mm

adidas

SHOPPING CART #9

Graphite and pencil crayon on Bristol paper | 121 × 152 mm

TOYS Я US

**SHOPPING CART #13**

Graphite on Bristol paper | 159 × 184 mm

FIVE NYC

SHOPPING CART #14

Graphite on Bristol paper | 152 × 152 mm

SHOPPING CART #17

Graphite on Bristol paper | 191 × 178 mm

SAFEWAY

SHOPPING CART #19

Graphite on Bristol paper | 203 × 140 mm

SHOPPING CART #18

Graphite on Bristol paper | 165 × 140 mm

SHOPPING CART #15

Graphite on Bristol paper | 165 × 152 mm

**SHOPPING CART #12**

Graphite on Bristol paper | 197 × 146 mm

AARON PECK

# EVIDENT BELONGING

**FOR YEARS,** on Avenue des Gobelins in the 13th arrondissement of Paris, a man sheltered under the awning of an abandoned commercial storefront. He built himself a small structure using old beds as walls and a blanket as a door. On the mattress facing the street, he scrawled the phrase, "LE VIEL HOMME ET LA MER," a misspelled translation into French of the title of Ernest Hemingway's *The Old Man and the Sea*. I used to walk by his home and wonder what it was about the novel that inspired him. I recently found myself in that part of the French capital again. The elaborate nest is gone, including the graffitied wall-bed, though the man still stays nearby.

In his shopping cart drawings, Taizo Yamamoto depicts traces of similar mysteries in Vancouver. Known for his work with Yamamoto Architecture, the artist here produces a body of work that appears to supplement his day job, with images that seem to parallel the design and production of buildings. He treats the carts the way an architect might: their users, who are also the owners of their contents, are unidentified and absent, similar to how architectural drawings render the structure, not the inhabitant. And yet, however connected his work as an architect may be to his output as an artist, these pieces are independent and involve different concerns.

From 2005 to 2008, Yamamoto took walks around Vancouver, particularly in the downtown core, during which he noticed the many shopping carts of unhoused people. "I would walk through the city," he told me via email, "and be ready to photograph any carts that stood out as being particularly intricate or unique." He was careful to take snapshots while the carts were unattended or when their stewards were otherwise preoccupied. Back in his studio, the artist made drawings from the pictures. This series, which renders these repurposed vernacular structures, then focuses on the particular gatherings of objects collected in them. All cropped in the same way, the compositions are uniform, consisting of the carts only in side profile, each pencil-drawn in the same method. In some, select details are coloured, such as the blue plastic of a Toys "R" Us cart and the pink floral print of an umbrella, although the majority remain uncoloured, leaving them with a forensic quality.

At first glance, his work acts as a document of the ubiquitous yet often ignored form of ephemeral architecture found across Vancouver's urban landscape. But these pieces also present a nuanced appreciation of the shopping carts, especially in our era of economic disparity. Yamamoto's drawings attempt to address the contradictions in how we encounter these objects by providing his subjects a certain respect. These carts are, no doubt, a phenomenon that requires discretion to observe, because looking directly at the personal effects and shelter of an unhoused person breaches a tacit social contract. We avoid gawking at the interior domestic spaces of strangers, except the rich and famous, so it follows that we too should afford those who find shelter in public spaces the same respect. This means these structures are often avoided, even underappreciated. The drawings then give us the ability to reflect on the nuanced aesthetic appreciation of these objects. It feels particularly poignant during the current housing crisis, which finds large numbers of individuals without safe places to live. These works can give us pause to look at what we might turn our eyes away from in public. Yamamoto's use of colour further mimics how we look at the items contained within the carts. The rare pops of pink or blue produce an effect similar to those brief moments in real life when a detail in a cart catches our eye before our gaze shifts toward a neutral object of attention. More than a record, the drawings represent how we see these things.

The series' documentary quality, not to mention meticulous realism, calls to mind certain photographic artworks. Formal and thematic similarities exist with Walker Evans's *Beauties of the Common Tool*, a 1955 series in which the celebrated photographer presents his subjects in a direct and simple way, as well as the work of Bernd and Hilla Becher, whose studies of German factory buildings from the early 1960s onward provide the viewer with typologies of industrial architecture. A local reference emerges in the drawings' affinity to Stephen Waddell's *Man in Green Mask* (2009), a picture of a man wearing a bright-green Halloween mask pushing a blue plastic shopping cart in what appears to be the Downtown Eastside. Even if the two art forms are in dialogue here, they have different functions: one is the source while the other is the result.

As he walked around Vancouver, Yamamoto selected specific carts to photograph, ones he found visually interesting. But what details make something "particularly intricate or unique," to use his words? The drawings, in this case, provide the clues. They are the items that hint at the complex inner lives of their owners. One cart is full of mannequins, another stuffed with suitcases. A spare bicycle tire rests on the bottom rack of another while a hockey stick protrudes from its plastic-covered contents. Umbrellas abound. A carry-on bag hangs over the handle of another. One is so encumbered with garbage bags that the cart is no longer visible. One is almost entirely empty, except for a pile of empty cans, perhaps not even used to housed personal effects. Each one hints at a story, the plot of which remains unknown to us.

Back on Avenue des Gobelins, I often considered asking that man about his choice of words for the mattress barrier, but I always opted against it. In any case, something about Yamamoto's shopping carts reminds me of that shelter and its cryptic literary reference. They are evidence of private stories in plain view. Informed by both his training as an architect and photographic traditions, these drawings represent their subjects, in a time of widening inequality, with a certain curiosity and carefulness by keeping their mysteries unsolved.

# HEDGES

2008-2009

**HEDGE #1**

Graphite on Bristol paper | 275 × 78 mm

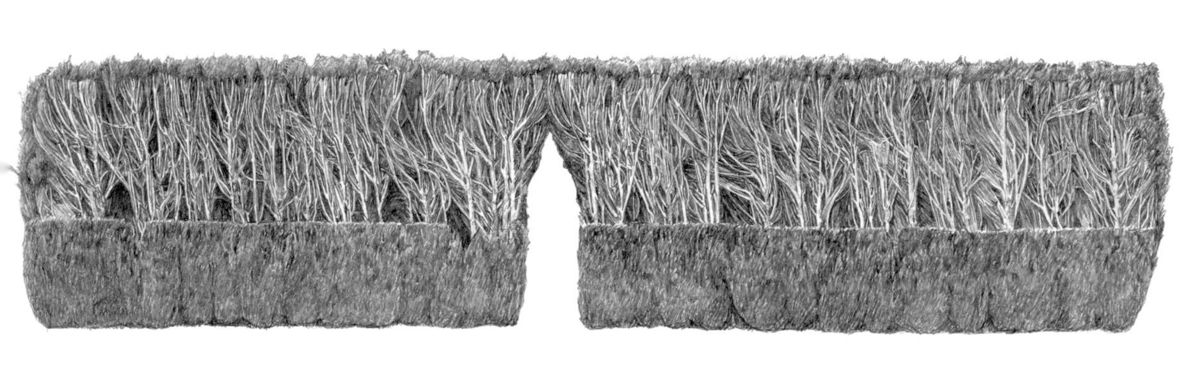

**HEDGE #2**

Graphite on Bristol paper | 283 × 59 mm

4329

## HEDGE #3

Graphite on Bristol paper | 283 × 59 mm

**HEDGE #4**

Graphite on Bristol paper | 283 × 59 mm

**HEDGE #5**

Graphite on Bristol paper | 283 × 59 mm

KEVIN CHONG

# THE PRIVACY HEDGE

## A SHORT STORY

**GROWING UP,** we lived next to the Seto family on the busy road that leads to the Oak Street Bridge. While our bay windows opened up to the traffic, the Setos lived behind laurel hedges that Mr. Seto, a serious-looking man who ran an electronics store on the east side, meticulously clipped twice a year with shears, on a stepladder. The hedges were as tidy and imposing as those of the Shaughnessy homes that I would see, decades later, when I briefly married into old Vancouver money.

Mr. Seto attending to the hedge was the only time we saw him. He and Mrs. Seto, often with their daughter, Candy, in her private-school uniform, always entered the house from the garage in the back lane. If we happened to be standing at our eat-in kitchen table, we could catch the tops of their heads.

To my chagrin, my parents owned a single twenty-one-inch colour TV and they often mused, in a sort of idle way that my brother found painfully cruel, about visiting the Setos' store to get a deal. "Would they even recognize us?" Mom asked rhetorically. "Of course they would," Dad answered. "But they would pretend they didn't."

Between their hedges they kept a tall gate on which they affixed a stencilled warning:

*Beware dog!*
*No tress-passer, no solicitor!*

There was no dog, my parents insisted. There was never a dog. It was just an empty threat. But my older brother, Damian, swore that he'd seen the dog in the Setos' backyard. "He's muzzled—that's why we can't hear him," my brother told me when he was eleven years old and I was eight. "Mr. Seto takes him outside at night to guard the house. I once saw him bite a guy who tried to come through the house." At night, before sleeping, I would press my head against the wall hoping I might hear a growl from Tiger—the name Damian had given the dog.

What I did hear coming from next door was a piano. Candy would practice regularly every day after she was driven home from her private school by Mrs. Seto. For several minutes she would warm up with scales. Then she would work her way through a composition, section by section, her playing wobbly on first try, before she halted and, summoning her wits, played again, brightly and confidently.

At precisely 4 PM, she would finish practicing. Occasionally, if the weather was good, she would ride her bike. If Damian and I were outside playing road hockey, she would push her bike past our net, eyes smiling at us and mouthing a hello, before she launched herself down the alley.

When I was twelve, Candy went missing. She was last seen on her bike, headed to the park to meet some friends, early on a spring evening. A few days later, we saw Mr. Seto wandering Oak Street, plastering the area with "Missing" posters. It was by studying one of those posters, which I ripped off a lamppost, that I first learned Candace Seto's given name and her height (five feet, one and a half inches) and weight (105 pounds). The poster featured a recent school photo: Candy in a forest-green pullover sweater that was part of her uniform.

The same picture was used in the newspapers and on TV during the murder trial. The Setos did not return home in the weeks that reporters parked outside their doorstep and even knocked on our door for comment. "They are a nice, hard-working family," my mother said into one microphone. "She was a sweet, quiet, studious girl." How did she know this? I suppose my mother wasn't lying; she merely extrapolated.

We never saw Mrs. Seto again. Whenever we saw anyone emerge from the garage into the backyard, it was Mr. Seto, his cheeks hollow and eyes shallow.

Mr. Seto stopped attending to the hedges, which lost their shape and grew out onto the street. Tickets from the city spilled out of the mailbox. One morning, we woke up to find that the hedges had been violently hacked back into the branches, up to six feet. Above that and behind into the yard, the hedges remained shaggy and green. The hedges, once beautiful, now resembled a mullet.

Through my teen years, the house was rented to students, normally only during the school year. For months at a time, it sat empty. The tidy backyard became overgrown. In my twenties, a "For Sale" sign went up in front of the house. "He knocked on the door with a bag of oranges for us. He wanted us to know they were finally selling the place," Dad told me, a few months before his heart attack. "We talked all of three minutes, but it was the longest conversation we ever had." The green of the hedges returned, but they were never tidy.

The last time I was back in Vancouver, I had time to stop at Mom's house. Orange construction fencing lined the yard of the Setos' former home, which was soon to be demolished so that the lot could be consolidated with other houses on the block and turned into townhomes. The hedges had already been removed and the house stood naked to passersby. I did not know that the house's exterior had a salmon-pink trim and grey stucco. I imagined how easy it would have been to see the Setos without the hedge, to hear their voices from inside—to hear Candy's piano playing.

At my insistence, I paid for double-glazed windows to be installed in my childhood home. My mother, now in her seventies and living alone, objected to the new windows as an extravagance, but she's pleased with the effects of the change. "I just sit here now," she says, watching the cars zoom by, "and enjoy the silence."

PLEASE CLOSE
THE GATE

# LION GATES

**LION GATE #1**

Graphite and pencil crayon on Bristol paper | 126 × 152 mm

**LION GATE #2**

Graphite and pencil crayon on Bristol paper | 135 × 113 mm

LION GATE #3

Graphite and pencil crayon on Bristol paper | 150 × 116 mm

**LION GATE #4**

Graphite and pencil crayon on Bristol paper | 130 × 118 mm

PLEASE CLOSE
THE GATE

**LION GATE #5**

Graphite and pencil crayon on Bristol paper | 200 × 117 mm

KEEP GATE
LOSED

LION GATE #6

Graphite and pencil crayon on Bristol paper | 111 × 125 mm

LION GATE #7

Graphite and pencil crayon on Bristol paper | 140 × 114 mm

**LION GATE #8**

Graphite and pencil crayon on Bristol paper | 128 × 115 mm

JACKIE WONG

# LUCKY LIONS

MY GRANDPARENTS SPENT the last decades of their lives in a Vancouver Special, the affordable, easy-to-build housing type popularized in the 1960s and known for its boxy exterior, low-pitched roof, and a kitchen and living room on both floors. My grandparents lived across the street from an elementary school, where they took me to kindergarten and around which they walked methodical laps after dinner, hands clasped behind their backs.

They were twenty-eight and thirty, living in Guangdong province, China, when the devastation of Mao Zedong's Great Leap Forward began. Along with my grandma's parents, they acquired black-market passports and started a new life in Lima, Peru. There, they operated and lived above a general store, learned Spanish, skimmed the surface of Roman Catholicism, and had three of their four children, including my dad. By the time they arrived in Vancouver, at the end of the same decade when Specials started to dot the local streets, they'd already lived so many lives. They were ready for things to get easier. By degrees, over the years, they did. They found jobs in a community that spoke their country dialect of Cantonese. They lived humbly. Their kids grew up and had kids. Their final home, which over the years housed three generations of family, reflected the unassuming stability they'd spent their lives working to create.

I didn't know that their style of house was called a Vancouver Special until I was in my twenties and they were both in decline. I never thought to ask them if they wanted something special to decorate their front gates, like a pair of lucky lion statues to guard their home. If I could ask them now, I can easily picture the answer. My grandfather would already be heading in the other direction, waving me away, shaking his head, uttering his tongue-clicking sigh of disapproval at any possibility of superfluousness.

But everyone else has them, I'd think to myself childishly. On some streets, it really seems like they do. According to my friend and colleague Christopher Cheung, whose work I edit in the local newsmagazine the *Tyee*, over ten thousand Vancouver Specials dot the city. Some blocks feature as many as ten in a row. The lion statues that stand in proud pairs at many of their front gates are as distinctive to this place as the homes that they guard.

The lions' presence as residential talismans of luck and courage speak to the aspirations and longings of generations who needed as much good fortune as they could find. The lions are especially numerous in neighbourhoods that historically have been home to working-class immigrant families. The lions vary in type: some lie flat on their bellies with their manes flowing across their backs; others hold a shield bearing a crest in a British colonial style; still others have Chinese design elements that feature a male lion with a paw positioned on a ball opposite a female lion holding its paw on a cub. Across these variations, two truths about the lions are perennial: they exist exclusively in pairs, and they always stand at a threshold. In the case of the lions guarding people's homes, they stand at a transitional juncture that separates private, personal space from the outside world. Never trendy but widely embraced, they speak to a universal desire to bless a new beginning. Doubly so if the arrival here has been preceded by struggle.

These blessings, made thousands of times over, spark swift business. The guardian lions and other statuary yard companions, such as concrete pine cones, bird baths, fruit bowls, and biblical figures, are made by one single family that has done this for years. The Tinucci family runs a bustling shop called Ital Decor on the easternmost end of Hastings Street in Burnaby. Joe Tinucci, who immigrated to Canada from Italy in 1956, founded the shop, which has operated in its Burnaby location since 1979. His sons Mario and Roberto have run the business since their father died in 2008. In the shop, a thick book of various post-topping ornaments helps customers make their selections. "Homeowners would come to our shop, choose what they wanted," Roberto told Cheung in 2023. "We would make the order: the lions, the balls, the pine cones, the pineapples."[1]

The lions at the gates of Vancouver houses are smaller take-home versions of those found at larger landmarks and institutions in town. A pair of carved granite lions was gifted to the City of Vancouver from the Port of Shanghai in 1995. The lions, which sit at the northern foot of Main Street at an entrance to the Port of Vancouver, are so placed to provide peace and prosperity at an important gateway. Farther west, in the downtown core, two large granite lions, sculpted by John Bruce and Timothy Bass in 1910, flank the steps of the former Vancouver courthouse, now the Vancouver Art Gallery.[2]

Most famously, a pair of 8.5-ton concrete lions stands at the Stanley Park entrance to the Lions Gate Bridge. The lions represent luck and courage, and receiving the commission was its own stroke of good fortune for longtime Vancouver resident, immigrant from Italy, and artist Charles Marega, who sculpted the statues in 1938. "Thank God I have work now," Marega wrote in a letter that year. "I would have preferred the lions to be in bronze or stone—but it has to be cheap—so they will be done in concrete which annoys me, as I could otherwise have made both Lions from one model. However I have to content myself to get work at all."[3]

Upon their installation in January 1939, workers placed silver coins under the lions' paws. There's an urban legend that one of the lions contains a box of memorabilia, including a pair of baby shoes.[4]

As statues built to greet travellers about to soar across Burrard Inlet on the first bridge to span Vancouver and the North Shore, it makes sense that the lions would be adorned with such universal symbols of auspiciousness.

My grandfather was an unyielding, practical man who brought his family across oceans, across languages, and into this improbable life on the West Coast of Canada. He didn't like to make a show of things. If he were here now and pressed by his grandchildren, maybe he'd go for a simpler decoration for the house, like the plain white balls that are the best-selling post ornament at Ital Decor today.

What my grandfather knew best was never said out loud. That people come here from all over the world to roll the dice on a new life. The odds are against them, just like they were for him, and they are betting on a future over which they ultimately have limited control. Much relies on luck.

## NOTES

1 Christopher Cheung, "How Vancouver Specials Got Their Guardians," *Tyee*, December 18, 2023, thetyee.ca/Culture/2023/12/18/How-Vancouver-Specials-Got-Guardians/.

2 See the City of Vancouver's Public Art Registry at covapp.vancouver.ca/PublicArtRegistry/HomePage.aspx.

3 Doreen Imredy, "Charles Marega, British Columbia's Forgotten Sculptor," *B.C. Historical News*, June 1975, www.library.ubc.ca/archives/pdfs/bchf/bchn_1975_06.pdf.

4 Glenn Tkach, "The Lions Gate Bridge—And the Lions Who Guard It," Forbidden Vancouver, May 15, 2019, forbiddenvancouver.ca/lions-gate-bridge-lions-guard/.

# ACKNOWLEDGEMENTS

**I WOULD LIKE TO THANK** my family, as well as Matthew Tichenor, for convincing me to turn the first drawing into a series. Thanks also to the Figure 1 Publishing team, and to Kevin Chong, Aaron Peck, and Jackie Wong for their thoughtful contributions. And special thanks to Jessica Guthrie.

# CONTRIBUTORS

**KEVIN CHONG** is the author of seven books of fiction and non-fiction, most recently the novel *The Double Life of Benson Yu*, which was a finalist for the 2023 Scotiabank Giller Prize and named a Best Book of Canadian Fiction by the CBC. His creative non-fiction and journalism have recently appeared in *Time*, Literary Hub, *Montecristo*, and the *Globe and Mail*. An associate professor at the University of British Columbia – Okanagan Campus, he lives in Vancouver with his family.

**AARON PECK** is the author of *Jeff Wall: North & West*, *Letters to the Pacific*, and *The Bewilderments of Bernard Willis*. Over the years, he has been a regular contributor to several contemporary art magazines, a writer of catalogue essays, and a speaker at museums. He currently writes for *Aperture* and the *Times Literary Supplement*.

**JACKIE WONG** is a writer and editor. She has published journalism on housing, racial equity issues, and drug policy. Wong works as a senior editor for the *Tyee*, an online newsmagazine for British Columbia. She lives in Vancouver with her family.

# ABOUT THE ARTIST

**TAIZO YAMAMOTO** was born in North Vancouver in 1975, the youngest of three siblings. His parents immigrated to Canada in the 1960s, his mother from East Germany and his father from Japan. Taizo began drawing at an early age, sketching on rolls of tracing paper provided by his father, Tomizo, a practicing architect. Taizo completed an architecture degree at McGill University, Montreal, and interned at Petersen Architects in San Francisco before moving to New York City to work for Frederic Schwartz Architects. In 2003, Taizo returned to Vancouver to take over his father's architectural practice, at which time he resumed drawing, beginning with the *Shopping Carts* (2005–2008) series. His artwork has since appeared in numerous national and international publications and exhibitions, and Yamamoto Architecture has grown from a staff of three to over thirty. Taizo lives in East Vancouver with his wife, who is a furniture designer, and their cat.

24 25 26 27 28 5 4 3 2 1



Cataloguing data is available from Library and Archives Canada
ISBN 978-1-77327-242-9 (hbk.)

Design by Jessica Sullivan | DSGN Dept.
Cover image: Taizo Yamamoto, *Shopping Cart #17*

Editing by Michael Leyne and Mélanie Ritchot
Copy editing by Jaclyn Arndt
Proofreading by Alison Strobel

Printed in Canada by Hemlock

Figure 1 Publishing Inc.
Vancouver BC Canada
www.figure1publishing.com

Figure 1 Publishing is located in the traditional, unceded territory of the xʷməθkʷəy̓əm (Musqueam), Sḵwx̱wú7mesh (Squamish), and səlilwətaɬ (Tsleil-Waututh) peoples.